White Elephant Gifts for Adults
Coloring Book
DON'T TELL THE BOSS

Welcome to Your Secret Creative Hideout!
Shhh... Don't Tell the Boss!
If you've picked up this book, you're probably seeking a creative getaway from the never-ending "symphony" of office keyboards and the mysterious disappearance of your favorite pen. Well, you're in the right place!
Inside these pages, you'll find a world where deadlines are just a myth, and the only meetings are between you, your colors, and a good chuckle. So, grab your coloring tools – be it crayons, markers, or the office supplies (we won't tell if you won't) – and let's add some color to those office blues.
Remember, what happens in the coloring book, stays in the coloring book.
Happy Coloring!

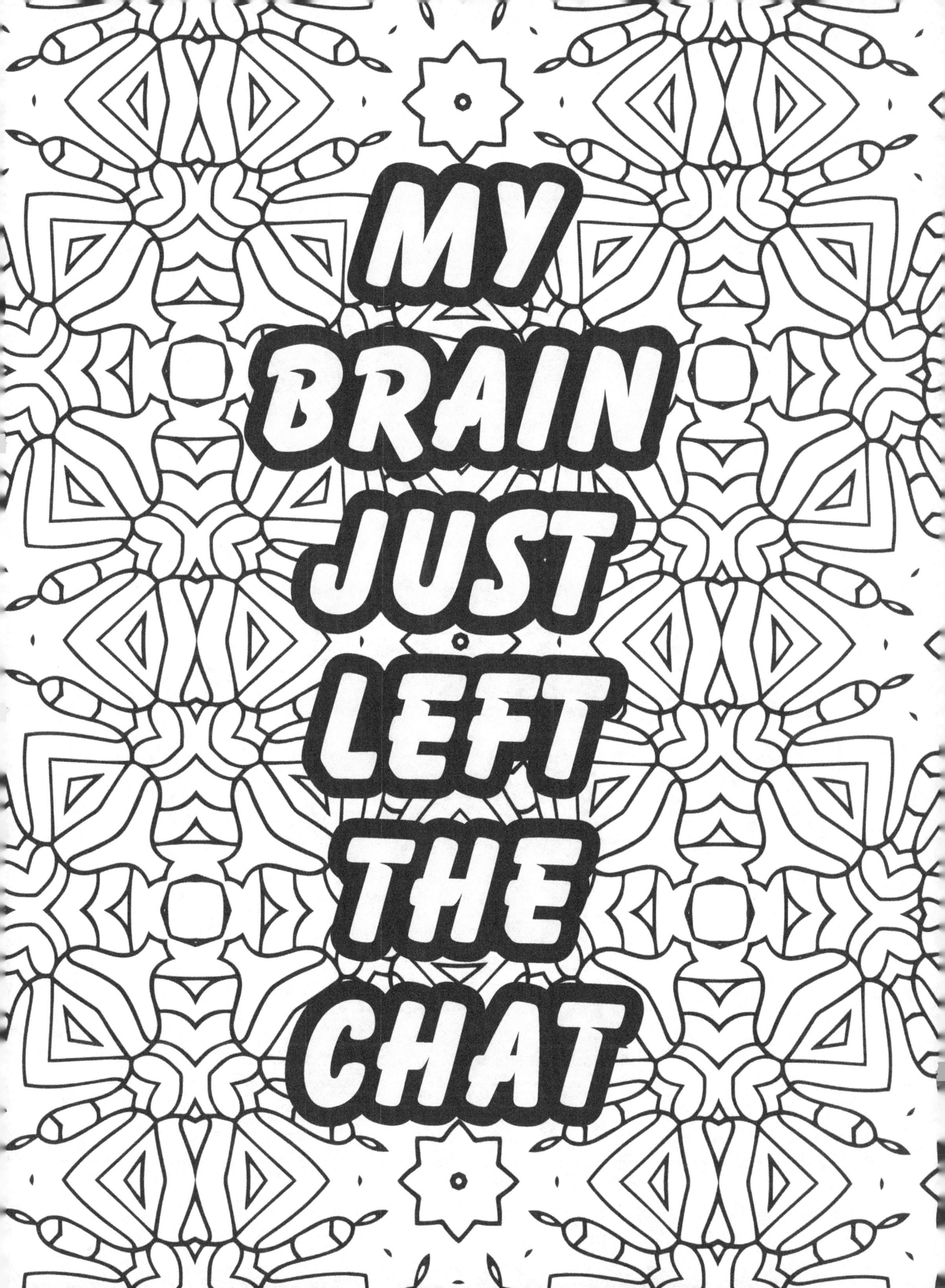

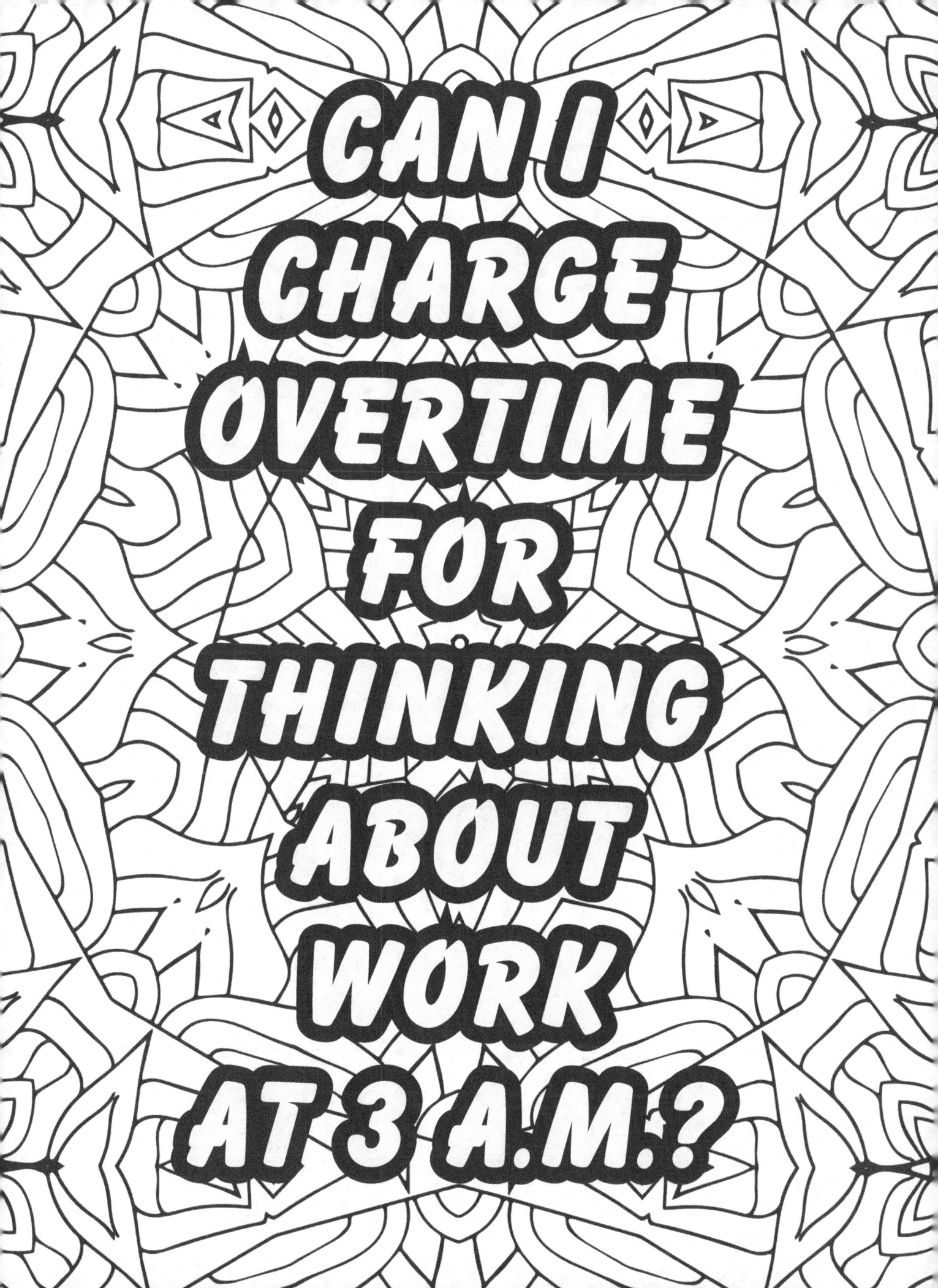

YOUR QUOTE HERE

YOUR QUOTE HERE →

Made in the USA
Monee, IL
28 November 2023